How Hound Became Happy

by Patricia A. Keeler
illustrated by Eldon Doty

Editorial Offices: Glenview, Illinois • New York, New York
Sales Offices: Reading, Massachusetts • Duluth, Georgia
Glenview, Illinois • Carrollton, Texas • Menlo Park, California

Hound wasn't happy. He had to do something. So Hound thought and thought.

He had an idea! Hound took out brushes and paper. He painted a picture of money. Then he reached into the picture.

Hound took out all the money.
He counted it.
Hound shouted, "I'm rich!"

Hound got a big house. But he still wasn't happy!

He looked around his big house. Hound was the only one there!

5

Hound had an idea! He knew what to do. Hound painted a new picture. It was a picture of a dog pound.

Hound jumped into the picture.
He let all the dogs out!

Hound took the dogs home with him. Now he wasn't lonely. He had lots of friends. But Hound still wasn't happy!

One dog was a grouch. He liked to sleep on the couch. He liked to sleep in the sun. He pouted when the clouds hid the sun.

The spotted dog barked too much. The little dogs cried. They cried louder and louder. "Ouch!" shouted Hound. "You are hurting my ears."

Then Hound had an idea!
He took out brushes and paper.
He painted a picture of grass.
Then he jumped into the picture.

Hound ran and ran. He played around in the grass. Then he curled up to rest. He was the picture of a happy dog!

Phonics for Families: This book features words that have the vowel sound heard in the beginning of *out* and two-syllable words such as *paper* and *became*. It also provides practice reading the high-frequency words *knew, picture, thought,* and *took*. Read the book together. Then ask your child to find words in the book that rhyme with *house*.

Phonics Skills: Vowel diphthong *ou* /ou/; Medial consonants (focus on decoding two-syllable words)

High-Frequency Words: *knew, picture, thought, took*